CLAPHAM AND STREATHAM TRAMWAYS

including Tooting and Earlsfield

John B Gent and John H Meredith

Series editor Robert J Harley

MP Middleton Press

--------- FEATURES IN LONDON *TRAMWAY CLASSICS* ---------

● Rolling Stock

A class. LCC	**Southwark and Deptford**
B class. LCC/Bexley	**Greenwich and Dartford**
B type MET	**Stamford Hill**
Barking cars	**Ilford and Barking**
Bexley cars.	**Greenwich and Dartford**
Bluebird. LCC car 1	**Camberwell and West Norwood**
C class. LCC	**Victoria and Lambeth**
Cable cars	**Clapham and Streatham**
Croydon cars	**Croydon's Tramways**
C type MET/LT	**Barnet and Finchley**
D class. LCC	**Wandsworth and Battersea**
Dartford cars	**Greenwich and Dartford**
East Ham cars	**East Ham and West Ham**
Erith cars	**Greenwich and Dartford**
E class. LCC/LT	**Aldgate and Stepney**
E1 class. LCC/LT	**Lewisham and Catford**
E1 cars 552-601. LCC/LT	**Hampstead and Highgate**
E1 cars 1777 - 1851 LCC/LT	**Clapham and Streatham**
E3 class. LCC/LT	**Camberwell and West Norwood**
E3 class. Leyton/LT	**Walthamstow and Leyton**
Experimental Tramcars MET/LUT/LT	**Barnet and Finchley**
F class. LCC	**Embankment and Waterloo**
G class. LCC	**Embankment and Waterloo**
G type MET/LT	**Stamford Hill**
Gravesend & Northfleet cars	**North Kent**
H class (works). LCC/LT	**Eltham and Woolwich**
H type MET/LT	**Stamford Hill**
Horse cars. North Met./LCC	**Aldgate and Stepney**
HR2 class. LCC/LT	**Camberwell and W Norwood**
Ilford cars	**Ilford and Barking**
L class (works). LCC/LT	**Holborn and Finsbury**
L/1 class (works) LCC/LT	**Clapham and Streatham**
Leyton cars	**Walthamstow and Leyton**
LT car 2	**Wandsworth and Battersea**
LUT car 341	**Kingston and Wimbledon**
M class. LCC/LT	**Greenwich and Dartford**
Petrol electric cars. LCC	**Southwark and Deptford**
SMET cars	**Croydon's Tramways**
T type. LUT	**Kingston and Wimbledon**
Trailer cars LCC	**Clapham and Streatham**
Walthamstow cars	**Walthamstow and Leyton**
West Ham cars	**East Ham and West Ham**

● Miscellaneous

Advertising on tramcars	**Aldgate and Stepney**
Conduit system	**Embankment and Waterloo**
Power supply	**Walthamstow and Leyton**
Request stops	**Victoria and Lambeth**
Section boxes	**Eltham and Woolwich**
Track layouts - single & loops	**Stamford Hill**
Track Construction and Maintenance	**Barnet and Finchley**
Tram tours	**Holborn and Finsbury**

Published July 1997

ISBN 1 873793 97 9

© Middleton Press 1997

Design - Deborah Goodridge

Published by Middleton Press
Easebourne Lane
Midhurst
West Sussex
GU29 9AZ
    Tel: 01730 813169
    Fax: 01730 812601

Printed & Bound by Biddles Ltd
    Guildford and Kings Lynn

CONTENTS

Brixton	1
Streatham	17
Norbury	35
Streatham to Tooting	40
Summerstown and Garratt Lane	66
Stockwell	73
Clapham	75
Balham	94
Tooting	108
Long Road and Cedars Road	112
Rolling Stock:	
Cable Cars	116
Trailer Cars	118
"Clapham" E/1 Class	120
Works Cars Class L/1	121

INTRODUCTION AND ACKNOWLEDGEMENTS

This volume completes the series of *Tramway Classics* devoted to London's tramways south of the River Thames. In the early 1930s, at the peak of tramway operation in the area described in this volume, there was not one actual track terminus, since all routes traversed Clapham, Steatham and Tooting and then penetrated into the areas covered by the five adjacent volumes as shown on the map. Nineteen routes served this part of South London and only two (10 and 32) regularly terminated inside the area, although many short workings were provided, particularly in peak hours.

Those readers who wish to acquire further knowledge of the development of tramways in the area are recommended to read *London County Council Tramways Volume 1 - South London* by E.R.Oakley, also *The Wheels Used To Talk To Us* - the reminiscences of Stan Collins as recounted to Terry Cooper, gives a fascinating personal view of tramway operations in the locality.

The authors' thanks go to Terry Russell and Roy Hubble for the tramcar drawings, to Ted Oakley, Derek Bayliss and Brian Salter for permission to use some of their drawings, and to B.J "Curly" Cross and Pat Loobey for their general assistance and the loan of a number of photographs from their collections. Thanks must also go to all those photographers and postcard publishers whose names, where known, are given in the text and without whom this book would not have been possible. The timetables are from World War II and are reproduced by permission of London Transport Museum.

GEOGRAPHICAL SETTING

There are no dramatic physical features in the area, but the London clay generally rises very gradually about 100 ft./ 30 metres from Brixton towards Streatham, with a lesser fall thence to the River Graveney which forms the Croydon boundary at Norbury. There is a gradual rise from Stockwell to Clapham Common, and then a corresponding fall through Balham to Tooting and the valley of the River Wandle. The only hills of note are in Cedars Road, the long gradual climb of Brixton Hill and some short, but quite steep, sections in Streatham High Road and Balham Hill. The route from Southcroft Corner through Tooting and Earlsfield to Wandsworth following the Rivers Graveney and Wandle is virtually level throughout.

HISTORICAL BACKGROUND

The two main roads south of London, now the A23 and A3, were both built originally by the Romans. The Surrey villages of Clapham, Streatham (pronounced "Strettam") and Tooting were for centuries isolated from London by large commons, market gardens and farmland. Clapham, being the nearest to London, became a popular place of residence from the late 17th century and still possesses some fine Georgian houses. The area south of Streatham Park achieved some cultural notoriety when the country home of Henry and Hester Thrale used to receive some of the most famous men of letters of the 18th century - noted visitors included Dr.Johnson, Boswell, Garrick and Goldsmith. Streatham and Tooting remained rural for longer, though both served as a retreat for prosperous London merchants who had large houses there. However, London began to spread outwards and suburban development had largely engulfed the area by the late 19th century. Today the commons of Clapham, Streatham, Tooting Bec and Wandsworth remain as green reminders of a more rural past.

The horse drawn passenger tramway era began when the Metropolitan Street Tramways line from Kennington, The Horns, to Brixton, Gresham Road, opened in May 1870; the route was extended to Brixton, Water Lane in August 1871. Meanwhile the same company had opened a line from Kennington to Stockwell in December 1870, which was later extended to the Plough, Clapham in May of the following year. The Metropolitan Street Tramways Company soon amalgamated with another South London tramway, the Pimlico, Peckham and Greenwich to form the London Tramways Company. In 1888 the Clapham route was extended, first to Nightingale Lane (July), then to Tooting Bec Road (December), and finally to Tooting, Totterdown in 1890. In the same year an Act was passed enabling the company to convert the section between Kennington and Brixton, Water Lane to cable traction, and to extend it up Brixton Hill to Streatham, Telford Avenue. In spite of the long drag up Brixton Hill the line is believed to have opened with horse traction for a few months, but cable operation started to Water Lane in December 1892, and to Telford Avenue in 1893. An extension to Streatham Village was authorised in 1894 and opened in 1895.

The whole area, previously part of Surrey, was included in the newly established London County Council (LCC) in 1888. In January 1889 the LCC purchased the London Tramways Company and the cable line was subsequently closed for conversion to electric operation in April 1904. Meanwhile the Stockwell to Clapham and Tooting service was converted to electric operation and this section opened in 1903. There had been long deliberation on the electrification system. London did not enjoy the autonomous authority exercised by county boroughs in other parts of the country, and the LCC was subject to the whims of several local boroughs who thought the street furniture associated with the tried and tested overhead line system would disfigure their environment. Hence the extremely expensive conduit system was adopted - this is described fully in companion volume *Southwark and Deptford Tramways*.

In 1905 the Clapham Road line was extended from Totterdown to Defoe Road, Tooting Broadway, and in 1907 the rails reached the county boundary at the south end of Tooting High Street, where they met the tracks of the London United Tramways (LUT) route to Wimbledon. In 1906 the tramway along Garratt Lane linking Wandsworth and Tooting had opened and a further extension in 1907 brought the line along Mitcham Road to meet the South Metropolitan Electric Tramways (SMET) terminus at Tooting Junction. The Streatham cable line was converted to electric traction and in 1909 was extended as far as Norbury, the northern terminus of Croydon Corporation Tramways. South of Streatham Station, the LCC employed the cheaper and more conventional overhead system of current collection. In 1910 the line linking Streatham and Tooting via Mitcham Lane and Southcroft Road was opened, and conduit tracks were also inaugurated in Long Road and Cedars Road. No more tramways were opened in the area, although at Wandsworth the hitherto isolated route from Putney to Harlesden was connected to tracks at the northern end of Garratt Lane in 1915, and in

1921 a link eastwards along Wandsworth High Street to the former terminus at East Hill was opened.

The speed of laying tramways was not matched by correspondingly swift negotiations with neighbouring tramway operators over the provision of through services. However, in 1926, with motor bus competition becoming ever more serious, through running commenced at two points on the LCC/Surrey boundary: at Norbury a joint LCC/Croydon Corporation service was inaugurated between Embankment and Purley, at Tooting Junction LCC cars began working over SMET metals to Mitcham. Four years earlier there had been a link up at Merton and the LCC had taken over operation of the LUT section to Wimbledon. A Sunday service was operated over LUT rails right through to Hampton Court until conversion of the LUT routes to trolleybus operation in 1931. Finally, at Summerstown where the LUT had continued to operate a short isolated route since 1922, the LCC took over full working in 1931 and introduced a Wimbledon to Hop Exchange via Summerstown service.

Following the formation of the London Passenger Transport Board in 1933, route 30 (Harlesden to Tooting Junction) was extended to West Croydon and this marked the final improve-ment to the area's tramway services. However, with the rehabilitation programme and the transfer of more modern cars following the introduction of trolleybuses elsewhere, there was a considerable improvement in the rolling stock. Tram drivers at last had windscreens to protect them.

The trolleybus conversion involved abandonment of tramway operation along Garratt Lane and south of Amen Corner in 1937. The intervention of World War II prevented the further planned conversion and gave the tramways an extended lease of life. After the War, buses were the order of the day and the Clapham Road services succumbed on 6th January 1951, while the last trams ran through Streatham with the conversion of routes 16 and 18 on 7th April 1951.

Summary of Services in June 1933

2 Wimbledon Station-Tooting-Clapham-Kennington-Embankment via Westminster/Blackfriars

2A Streatham Library-Tooting-Clapham-Kennington-Embankment via Westminster/Blackfriars

4 Wimbledon Station-Tooting-Clapham-Kennington-Embankment via Blackfriars/Westminster

4A Streatham Library-Tooting-Clapham-Kennington-Embankment via Blackfriars/Westminster

6 Mitcham Cricket Green-Tooting-Clapham-Kennington-City

8 Victoria-Stockwell/Clapham/Tooting/Streatham/Brixton/Stockwell-Victoria

10 Tooting Broadway-Streatham-Brixton-Kennington-City

12 Tooting Junction-Wandsworth-Battersea-St.George's Circus-Hop Exchange

14 Wimbledon Station-Merton-Summerstown-Wandsworth-Battersea-Embankment-Hop Exchange

16 Purley-Croydon-Streatham-Brixton-Embankment via Westminster/Blackfriars

18 Purley-Croydon-Streatham-Brixton-Embankment via Blackfriars/Westminster

20 Victoria-Stockwell/Brixton/Streatham/Tooting/Clapham/Stockwell-Victoria

22 Tooting Broadway-Streatham-Brixton-Embankment via Westminster/Blackfriars

24 Tooting Broadway-Streatham-Brixton-Embankment via Blackfriars/Westminster

30 Tooting Junction-Wandsworth-Putney-Hammersmith-Harrow Road (Scrubs Lane)

31 Hackney Station - Kingsway Subway - Battersea - Wandsworth (extended on Sundays Wandsworth - Tooting Junction and Hackney Station - Leyton Bakers Arms)

32 Clapham Common-Cedars Road-Chelsea Bridge

34 King's Road, Chelsea-Clapham Junction-Cedars Road-Clapham-Stockwell-Camberwell Green

89 Acton-Hammersmith-Putney (extended on Saturday afternoons to Wandsworth and Tooting Junction)

/ indicates sections of route operated in one direction only

Services 2A and 4A were worked in combination with services 22 and 24; the service numbers on the cars were changed as required. All four of these services operated during Monday to Saturday rush hours only. All the other services listed above operated on a daily basis.

There were a number of regular rush hour short workings on services 2, 4, 16 and 18. These were designated 2EX, 4EX, 16EX and 18EX. The cars displayed EX stencils on their side service number indicators (see picture 7). A few other short workings outside the area under review operated at certain times, e.g. service 10 was cut back from City to St.George's Church on Saturday evenings, some cars on service 30 were extended from Harrow Road to Craven Park on Mondays to Fridays, and Wembley on Monday to Friday rush hours and on Saturdays.

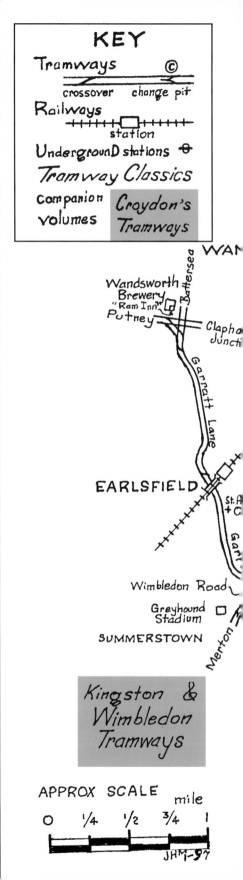

TRAMWAY LAYOUT
AS AT JUNE 1933

N

Wandsworth &
Battersea Tramways

Vauxhall

STOCKWELL

Kennington

Kennington

Chelsea Bridge

Vauxhall

Clapham Road

"Swan"

Camberwell

Clapham
Junction

Cedars Road

Clapham High Street

Clapham
North

Long Road

"Plough Inn"

Clapham
Depot

Brixton Road

BRIXTON

Clapham
Common

South Side

Water
Lane

Herne
Hill

CLAPHAM

Camberwell &
West Norwood
Tramways

Nightingale Lane

Clapham
South

Balham Road Hill

Brixton Hill

Brixton Hill
Depot

BALHAM

Telford Avenue
Depot

Marius
Road
Depot

Balham High Road

Streatham Hill

ing Bec) Trinity
Road

Streatham
Hill

STREATHAM

Upper Tooting Rd

TOOTING

Streatham High Road

Streatham Library

St. Leonard's Church

Defoe
Road

Totterdown
Street

Mitcham Lane

Tooting
Broadway

ring High Street

Amen Corner

Mitcham Road

Southcroft Road

Streatham

Tooting
Junction

Mitcham

Southcroft
Corner

Streatham
Common

Emmanuel Church

Streatham High Road

ERTON

NORBURY

Hermitage
Bridge
(River Graveney)

Croydon

Croydon's
Tramways

THE SURREY IRON RAILWAY

Well before the rapid development of the Garratt Lane area in the late 19th and early 20th centuries, the world's first public railway, the horse drawn Surrey Iron Railway (1803-1846), had followed much of what is now Garratt Lane between Wandsworth and Summerstown. The railway was a freight tramroad linking the River Thames at Wandsworth with Croydon and serving the industries along the River Wandle. The accompanying map is reproduced by kind permission of Brian Salter from *Retracing the First Public Railway* by Derek A.Bayliss (Living History Publications 1981).

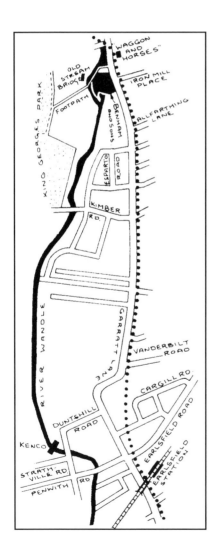

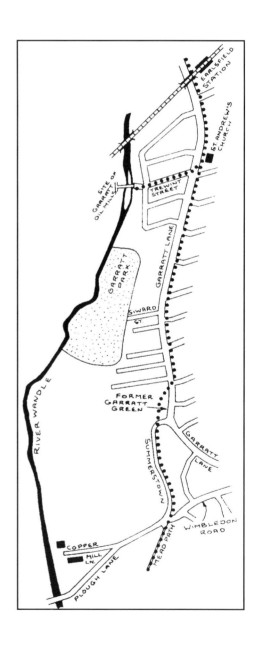

BRIXTON

1. Bon Marche and Quin & Axtens' stores, together with good public transport, helped make Brixton one of South London's main shopping centres. Cable car 911 is being hauled along Brixton Road towards one of the Thames bridges; at Kennington the cable gripper will be disengaged and horses will take over for the rest of the journey.   (John B.Gent Coll.)

2. This postcard view was sent in November 1912 and we note that conduits for electric conductors have replaced the cable appparatus. In the days before route numbering, E/1 car 830 is on its way to Westminster Bridge, whilst some E class cars without trolley poles and a London General Omnibus Company (LGOC) B type bus can also be seen.   (John B.Gent Coll.)

3.   As electrification developed elsewhere, the LCC considered hauling B class electric trams to Streatham by cable. Their weight proved too much for the system and the cable car route was closed on 5th April 1904. In a mammoth operation, the section from Kennington as far as Water Lane was reconstructed and reopened using electric traction on 30th May 1904. B class car 194 is about to reverse at this temporary terminus, probably on the opening day.   (J.H.Price Coll.)

4.   Electric operation was extended to Streatham Village on 19th June 1904. In this scene facing north, a little to the south of Water Lane, E/1 car 1034 is heading for Victoria in about 1910. (John B.Gent Coll.)

5. The horse tramway from Westminster Bridge had reached Water Lane in 1871. Cable haulage from Kennington was adopted in 1892 and the route was extended to Telford Avenue in 1893. From 1904 to 1951 electric traction was used. In this leisurely scene from the earliest days of the electric era, B class car 180 has passed Water Lane on its way towards Streatham and is about to climb Brixton Hill. (John B.Gent Coll.)

6. In this 1950 view parts of Brixton Hill are still flanked by long tree lined front gardens. Clapham based E/1 car 1843 on route 20 is followed by Feltham car 2129 on route 18 and a well filled RT bus is one of the few other vehicles on the road. (John H.Meredith)

7. E/1 car 1741 has reached the top of Brixton Hill on a short working to Norbury. Note that the front stencil displays route 16A whilst the side stencil shows EX. The year is about 1930. (John H.Meredith Coll.)

8. Brixton Hill Depot, although built to house trailer cars, was opened in 1924 to stable part of Telford Avenue Depot's electric car fleet. The rails remained unbonded until about 1927, hence the double overhead, and E/1s 1727 to 1776 were adapted to use both positive and negative wires when entering or leaving the depot. Conduit ploughs were released and taken up at the depot entrance. This was the only LCC depot to be equipped with a track fan rather than a traverser. A former Croydon Corporation tram is passing the depot on 12th July 1946, while a track repair gang labours on one of the depot turnouts.   (G.F.Ashwell)

9. The inside of the depot in 1949 presented a melancholy spectacle as four E/1s and ex-West Ham car 329 wait their turn to be broken up. Operational Feltham cars can be seen on the extreme left, whilst on the right the car with the bent trolley pole is snow broom 033.   (John H.Meredith Coll.)

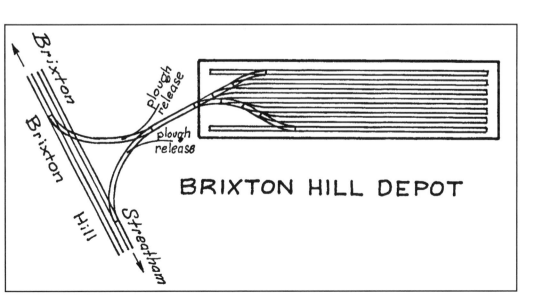

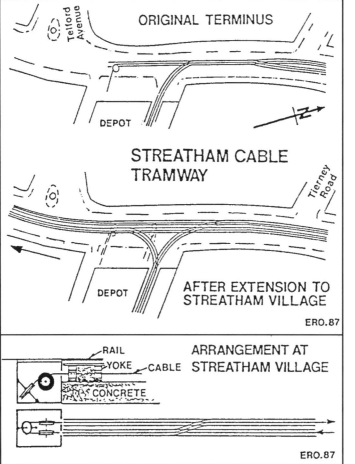

ORIGINAL TERMINUS

Telford Avenue

DEPOT

STREATHAM CABLE TRAMWAY

Tierney Road

AFTER EXTENSION TO STREATHAM VILLAGE

DEPOT

ERO.87

RAIL

YOKE — CABLE

CONCRETE

ARRANGEMENT AT STREATHAM VILLAGE

ERO.87

10. Cable car 922, having climbed Brixton Hill, has just entered Streatham Hill, and is seen close to Christchurch Road. The tram is proceeding at the sedate cable speed of 8 mph/13 kmh! This postcard view was franked on 19th August 1905, but cable haulage had ceased over a year earlier.
(John B.Gent Coll.)

Reproduced from *LCC Tramways Volume 1 (London Tramways History Group)*, courtesy of E.R. Oakley.

11. The nerve centre of the cable car system was at Telford Avenue where the power house and depot were situated. The route terminated outside the depot when it opened in 1893, but it was extended to Streatham Village in 1895. This scene shows a dummy (non-passenger tractor unit, connected by a grip mechanism to the underground cable) about to pull a passenger car from the depot before the extension was opened. (John H.Meredith Coll.)

12. Inside the depot cars were drawn up a ramp on to a traverser, also cable operated, to enable the trams to be dispersed over a number of storage tracks. Traversers later found favour with the LCC for their electric car depots. Track fans would not have been practicable for cable or conduit operation. Steam driven cable winding drums were housed in a parallel building to the right of the depot. (John H.Meredith Coll.)

13. In 1905 a new electric car depot was built on the site of the cable car shed and engine house. To increase capacity, a second shed was added on the south side and this was opened in 1912. In this view ex-LUT Feltham car 2137 is outside the original part of the depot in about 1938; note the contrast in architectural styles between the depot and Frederick Gibberd's Pullman Court of 1935. The forty-six LUT Felthams (2120-2165) were fitted with conduit gear and transferred to Telford Avenue on the demise of the Uxbridge route 7 in 1936. The fifty-four MET Felthams (2066-2119), already conduit equipped for their North London duties, followed in 1938, together with just one of the three experimental Felthams, car 2167. (Bob Mayes)

14. Feltham car 2123 is rostered on a short EX working to Croydon and is approaching Telford Avenue on 6th January 1951. Any one of about six crossovers covering a distance of two miles across Croydon could have been the destination - it is to be hoped that the conductor will explain to intending passengers at which exact spot, ranging from West Croydon to the Red Deer, they'll all end up! E/3 car 1918 is working route 10, the final day for this service before bus route 95 takes over. Bus stop signs are already in place and temporary stop signs have been provided for tram passengers, although the Croydon and Purley tram route will enjoy another three months of operation. (John H.Meredith)

15. Another scene on 6th January 1951 with E/3 car 1927 entering the depot as Feltham car 2146 emerges. This vehicle is probably only bound for Brixton Hill Depot as, in common with most of the other ex-LUT trams, it was destined to stay in London until April. Meanwhile, all but one of the remaining ex-MET cars were taken out of service pending transhipment to Leeds. Although the London system was already doomed, the LT recruitment notice on the left still says that tram conductors are wanted.   (John H.Meredith)

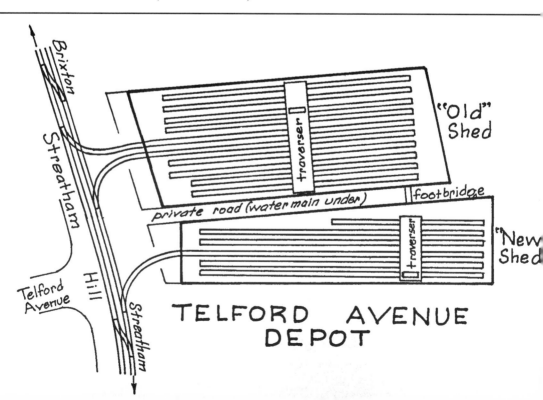

TELFORD AVENUE DEPOT

16. On 13th April 1947 E/1 car 1038 is framed in the single track entrance to the "new" shed. This car was the first of some 160 to be "rehabilitated" by London Transport between 1935 and 1937, but unlike most of its successors it retains route number stencils. A narrow space between the two car sheds at Telford Avenue had to be maintained due to the presence of a large water main, but a footbridge connection was provided. (John H. Meredith)

ALL NIGHT TRAM ROUTE	Tooting - Streatham - Brixton - Westminster - Savoy Street													
	Tooting - Clapham - Elephant - Blackfriars - Savoy Street													
	SATURDAY NIGHT, SUNDAY MORNING EXCEPTED													
	Via Streatham, Brixton & Westminster							Via Balham, Clapham & Blackfriars						
TOOTING BDY Stn., Und.	....	....	....	1 13		4 43	5 23	5 43	6 13	....	....	....	1 23		4 53	5 53	6 23
Streatham St. Leonards Ch.	..	..	..	1 25		4 55	5 35	5 55	6 25	..	..	..	..		..	..	..
Streatham Hill Telford Avenue	12 0	12 30	1 0	1 30	Then every 30 mins. until	5 0	5 40	6 0	6 30	12 6	12 36	1 6	1 36	Then every 30 mins. until	5 6	6 6	6 36
Clapham Common Stn., Und.	12 16	12 46	1 16	1 46		5 16				12 16	12 46	1 16	1 46		5 16		
Westminster Stn., Und.	12 25	12 55	1 25	1 55		5 25											
Elephant and Castle	....	....	....	....		....				12 22	12 52	1 22	1 52		5 22		
Blackfriars John Carpenter St.	....	....	....	....		....				12 30	1 0	1 30	2 0		5 30		
EMBANKMENT Savoy Street	12 30	1 0	1 30	2 0		5 30				12 33	1 3	1 33	2 3		5 33		
	Via Westminster, Clapham and Balham							Via Blackfriars, Brixton and Streatham						
EMBANKMENT Savoy Street	12 33		4 3	4 33	5 3	5 33				12 30		5 30					
Blackfriars John Carpenter St.	..		..	..	..	..				12 35		5 35					
Elephant and Castle	..	Then every 30 mins. until	..	..	..	..				12 43	Then every 30 mins. until	5 43					
Westminster Station, Und.	12 40		4 10	4 40	5 10	5 40				..		..					
Clapham Common Stn., Und.	12 50		4 20	4 50	5 20	5 50				12 50		5 50					
Kennington Gate	12 59		4 29	4 59	5 29	5 59				..		..					
Streatham Hill Telford Avenue	....		....	....	....	....				1 5		6 5					
Streatham St. Leonards Ch.	..		..	..	..	..				1 10		6 10					
TOOTING BDY. Stn. Und.	1 13		4 43		5 43	6 13				1 23		6 23					

ALL NIGHT TRAM ROUTE	Battersea - Vauxhall - Westminster - Blackfriars	See page 13
ALL NIGHT TRAM ROUTE	Clapham Junction - Vauxhall - Westminster Station - Borough	See page 11
ALL NIGHT TRAM ROUTE	New Cross Gate - Camberwell Green - Elephant - Savoy Street	See page 17

STREATHAM

←————

17. Feltham car 2126 is passing Streatham Hill Theatre on 15th June 1949, while an STL bus on route 118 is making its circuitous way from Morden to Clapham Common. This section of Streatham Hill had been widened on the west side before the Second World War and the opportunity was taken after the war to provide a tramway loading island.   (John H.Meredith)

19. The conduit system was particularly vulnerable to snow and ice; car 022 is doing its best to clear the tracks along Streatham Hill on 21st February 1948. Despite their use in adverse weather conditions, snow broom cars were never fitted with windscreens. These vehicles had been converted from B class passenger cars, and 022 later achieved fame as the one selected for preservation. It has now been beautifully restored to almost its original open top condition, and it can be seen at the National Tramway Museum in Crich, Derbyshire. There it carries its earlier number 106 and for practical purposes has "normal" stairs and a trolley pole; compare with picture 3. (Vic Jones)

←————

18. Looking south along Streatham Hill, the colonnaded facade of the Gaumont Cinema is on the right, and in the middle distance stands the unpretentious Streatham Hill Station which marks the end of the widened carriageway. Two tramcars, two buses and just a handful of other vehicles create this typical early postwar scene. (John H.Meredith Coll.)

20. Photographed around 1907 and long before the road widening, a top covered C class car is proceeding north from Streatham Hill Station, followed in leisurely fashion by a splendid horse drawn carriage. The car is in its intermediate stage: top covered, but still with reversed stairs and open balconies. (John B.Gent Coll.)

21. Some five years later than the previous view and E/1 car 1004 is observed approaching Streatham Hill Station. It is bound for the then terminus of Norbury. Closely following the E/1 car is an E class tram probably bound for Tooting; this vehicle has not been equipped with a trolley pole.   (John B.Gent Coll.)

22. South of Streatham Hill Station a section of the High Road was widened on the east side and this allowed space for another loading island. At night, this location was illuminated by two Wandsworth Borough Council gas lamps. The leading tramcar is ex-Walthamstow car 2057; behind is former Croydon car 397, and in the distance is an ex-LCC E/1 on route 8. The forlorn building on the left is the long closed Golden Domes Cinema.   (John H.Meredith)

23. On 21st June 1949 two trams on route 10 pass at speed near the Astoria Cinema in Streatham High Road. Both cars are operating from Norwood Depot; on the left is E/3 car 1938, and on the right is London's newest tram, car 2. The latter was a virtually new tramcar in 1935 and it is featured in companion volume *Wandsworth and Battersea Tramways*. (John H.Meredith)

24. Outside Streatham Library and the tram conveys its own stop sign! The driver of former Croydon car 393 alights from his platform with a temporary sign as the usual location is obstructed by repair work. Austerity and clothes rationing don't seem to have dealt too harshly with the lady making her way past the obstruction. (John H.Meredith)

25. The electric tram terminus remained at Streatham Library from 1904 to 1909 and was at the same location as the former cable car terminus. Here C class car 228 stands ready to depart for Blackfriars; this postcard view was sent in May 1908.   (John B.Gent Coll.)

26. The junction of the Croydon and Tooting routes was at Streatham, St.Leonard's Church. On Sunday, 1st October 1950, E/3 car 202 is a newcomer to the area. The Battersea tram routes had been abandoned on the previous day and a number of these ex-Leyton cars were moved to Telford Avenue Depot to replace Felthams being sold to Leeds. The point lever on the extreme right controls the facing junction, and pointsmen, often light duty men, were employed for this somewhat tedious task.   (John H.Meredith)

27. A certain amount of stores movement was undertaken by tram until closure and here stores van 015 is travelling northwards to St.Leonard's Church from either Thornton Heath or Purley Depot. Most stores vans were purpose built, but car 015 was a conversion from C class car 273. A Daimler utilty bus follows. (K.Thorpe)

ROUTES 8/20 — Victoria - Clapham - Tooting - Streatham - Victoria

P.M. times are in heavy figures

Route 8, via Vauxhall Bridge Road, Vauxhall Bridge, South Lambeth Road, Clapham Road, Clapham High Street, Clapham Common, Balham High Road, Upper Tooting Road, Tooting High Street, return via Mitcham Road, Southcroft Road, Mitcham Lane, Streatham High Road, Streatham Hill, Brixton Hill, Stockwell Road, Vauxhall Bridge and Vauxhall Bridge Road. Route 20 operates in the reverse direction

RAILWAY STATIONS SERVED : Victoria, Vauxhall, Stockwell, Clapham SR, Clapham North, Clapham Common, Clapham South, Balham, Trinity Road, Tooting Broadway, Streatham Hill, Brixton

Service interval : Route 8 (via Clapham and Balham), WEEKDAYS 6-8 mins. (eve. 10 mins.), SUNDAY morn. 12 mins.; aft. and eve. 10 mins.   Route 20 (via Brixton and Streatham), WEEKDAYS 6-8 mins. (eve. 10 mins.), SUNDAY morn. 12 mins., aft. and eve. 10 mins.

	WEEKDAYS First					SUNDAY First					DAILY Last				
VICTORIA Clock Tower	...	...	5 56	6 48	...	...	...	7 14	8 19	...	...	10 25	10 31	...	...	...
Stockwell Swan	...	...	6 8	7 0	...	..	...	7 26	8 31	...	...	10 38	10 44	...	..	...
Clapham Common Station	5 1	...	6 14	...	...	..	7 26	7 31	...	...	...	10 45	...	...	..	..
Telford Avenue Streatham Hill	...	5 14	...	7 15	...	6 57	...	...	8 45	...	...	...	11 2	...	...	....
Streatham St. Leonards Church	...	5 19	...	7 20	...	7 2	...	...	8 50	...	...	...	11 7	...	...	....
Southcroft Road Mitcham Lane	...	5 26	...	7 27	...	7 7	...	...	8 56	...	...	...	11 14	...	...	...
TOOTING Broadway	...	5 17	5 33	6 27	7 33	7 14	7 39	7 44	9 2	...	...	11 1	11 21	...	...	...

											S&0 Last	MF			
TOOTING Broadway	5 19	6 21	...	c	..	...	7 16	7 42	7 44	...	9 37	9 45	9 47	11 1	11 21	...
Southcroft Road Mitcham Lane	...	6 27	...	...	..	..	...	7 22	...	7 50	...	9 44	...	...	11 8	...
Streatham St. Leonards Church	...	6 34	...	...	..	...	...	7 28	...	7 56	...	9 51	...	...	11 15	...
Telford Avenue Streatham Hill	...	6 39	...	...	..	...	...	†7 32	...	8 1	...	9 56	...	...	11 20	...
Clapham Common Station	5 35	...	...	...	...	6 55	...	7 55	...	...	...	10 1	10 3	...	...	11 37
Stockwell Swan	5 42	6 54	...	...	..	7 0	...	...	8 0	8 15	...	10 14	10 8	10 10	...	...
VICTORIA Clock Tower	5 54	7 6	...	...	..	7 12	...	...	8 12	8 27	...	10 27	10 21	10 23	...	...

MF—Monday to Friday.   S&0—Saturday and Sunday only.   *—Special early journey.
†—Time at Streatham Library.

28. In this delightful scene from about 1910, E/1 car 1018 has just taken up its plough and is climbing the short hill to St.Leonard's Church. (John B.Gent Coll.)

29. The plough change was situated opposite Gleneagle Road, just north of Streatham Station. Viewed from the change pit and facing north, both conduit and overhead can be seen, the latter having earthed guard wires over the power lines to protect telegraph apparatus should higher telephone wires fall. This practice was once quite widely adopted on British tramways.   (John B.Gent Coll.)

30. Although car 1 spent much of the Second World War delicensed in Telford Avenue Depot, it is seen here at Streatham change pit, probably in 1944. Note the wartime conductress, the masked headlamp and the white painted fender. The route number 18A denotes a short working; by this time only car 1 used this form, other types of car would show EX or 18X for such workings.
(V.E.Burrows)

31. Looking south along Streatham High Road from the change pit, Streatham Station can be seen behind the bus. Former Croydon car 388 is now "on conduit" and about to continue its journey only a week before closure of the route. Note the lights on the left hand pole to assist conductors where trolley poles were routinely raised. These lights could not be used during the wartime blackout and hoods with neon bulbs were fitted over the wire in their place. (John H.Meredith)

32. Close to Streatham Bus Garage on 4th March 1951, E/3 car 1930 is proceeding south along Streatham High Road. The 18 stencil has no doubt been produced as a stop gap after the influx of E/3s at Telford Avenue Depot. It is interesting to compare this stencil with the Croydon Corporation type in picture 31. (John H.Meredith)

33. Feltham car 2144 is seen at Streatham Common on 18th March 1950. This car never made it to Leeds as it was badly damaged in a fire at Brixton Hill Depot on 19th November 1950. Note the rather of austere tower of Emmanuel Church which dates from 1865. (John H.Meredith)

34. Beyond Streatham Common the High Road drops sharply to Norbury, and car 1906 is slowing to the compulsory stop at Heathdene Road. Note the fixed centre windows on the upper deck. This car was probably one of those in Thornton Heath Depot in 1944 when flying bomb damage resulted in many of its tramcars running without glazing for several days! Windows were later replaced, but the centre pairs of half drop windows were boarded up and later given fixed lights. (John H.Meredith

NORBURY

35. The LCC's Norbury route ended in a pair of sharp radius reverse curves. This view facing south shows two trams standing at the terminus which was originally equipped with scissors crossovers in both the LCC and Croydon areas.   (C.H.Price)

36. Soon after the July 1909 opening of the Norbury extension, E/1 car 1477 stands at the terminus. The board below the lower deck windows still confines the route to Streatham, but the notice on the upper deck invites passengers to CHANGE CARS AT NORBURY FOR THORNTON HEATH, CROYDON AND PURLEY. (R.J.Harley Coll.)

37. Bound for Purley on route 18, Feltham car 2123 is about to cross Hermitage Bridge over the River Graveney which formed the county boundary between London and Surrey. The undistinguished shops on the right have replaced the old timber clad buildings seen in the previous view. (John H.Meredith)

38. A short gap in the rails separated the LCC and Croydon systems when this photograph was taken in 1919, but, strangely, the overhead wires appear to be continuous. Unusually, Croydon Corporation car 38 and LCC car 1084 do not seem to be exchanging many passengers. (O.J.Morris)

39. The tracks were eventually connected and joint through services began on 7th February 1926. E/1 car 1248 is seen at "the terminus" on the first day of through running. Although incorrect, the location retained this colloquial name until after the trams ceased in 1951. (B.J.Cross Coll.)

STREATHAM TO TOOTING

40. The line from Streatham to Tooting opened in 1910, diverging from the Norbury extension at St.Leonard's Church. A few yards south of the junction, smartly painted E/1 car 1252 is on a route 8 working, while two people rest and enjoy the afternoon sunshine on 25th July 1948. (B.T.Cooke)

41. Mitcham Lane, along which the first part of the Tooting extension was routed, had narrow sections of carriageway, and two lengths of single track were laid to avoid road widenening costs. An E class tram is about to enter the first of these sections at Ambleside Avenue. (John B.Gent Coll.)

42. On 30th April 1950 former Walthamstow car 2049, northbound on route 8, is entering the Ambleside Avenue single track section while E/3 car 1920 is awaiting its turn to come south. Unlike some sections of single track, the conduit was also single, thereby enabling a tram to reverse if necessary.   (John H.Meredith)

43. E class car 549 makes its way over the second section of single track in Mitcham Lane, at Thrale Road. The meticulous photographer has noted the exact time: 3.30pm on 28th April 1917. (O.J.Morris)

ROUTE 22	Embankment - Vauxhall - Clapham - Tooting Broadway	
ROUTE 24	Embankment - Vauxhall - Brixton - Streatham - Tooting Bdwy.	P.M. times are in heavy figures

Via Victoria Embankment, Westminster Bridge, Lambeth Palace Road, Albert Embankment, South Lambeth Road, Route 22 via Clapham Road, Clapham High St., Clapham Common South Side, Balham Hill, Balham High Road, Upper Tooting Road, Mitcham Road, return via Southcroft Road, Mitcham Lane, Streatham High Road, Streatham Hill, Brixton Hill, Stockwell Road. (Route 24 in the reverse direction), South Lambeth Road, Albert Embankment, Lambeth Palace Road, Westminster Bridge, Victoria Embankment

RAILWAY STATIONS SERVED : Charing Cross, Westminster, Vauxhall, Stockwell, Clapham North, Clapham SR, Clapham Common, Clapham South, Balham, Trinity Road, Tooting Broadway, Streatham Hill, Brixton

Service interval : WEEKDAY PEAK HOURS, 10 minutes in each direction

	WEEKDAYS MORNING					MONDAY to FRIDAY AFTERNOON						SATURDAY AFTERNOON					
	First		Last			First			Last			First			Last		
SAVOY ST. *Embankment*	....	7 31	7 46	7 51	8 6	9 36	....	5 18	5 22	6 59	7 4	....	..	12 3	12 8	....	2 24	2 29	....	....
Vauxhall *Station*	..	7 42	7 57	8 2	8 17	9 47	...	5 29	5 33	7 10	7 15	..	12 14	12 19	...	2 35	2 40	..	..
Stockwell *Swan*		7 49	8 4	8 9	8 24	9 54	...	5 36	5 40	7 17	7 22		12 21	12 26	...	2 42	2 47	..	..
Clapham Common *Station*	6 37		8.10		8.30	10 0	3 59		5 46	7 23			12 32			2 53			
Streatham *St. Leonards Ch.*		8 9		8 29			†4 28	5 57			7 43		12 41			3 2			
Southcroft Rd. *Mitcham Lane*		8 16		8 36			4 36	6 4			7 50		12 48			3 9			
TOOTING BROADWAY	6 50	8 22	8 23	8 42	8 43		4 13	4 42	6 10	6 0	7 37	7 56	12 54	12 46		3 15	3 7		

	WEEKDAYS MORNING					MONDAY to FRIDAY AFTERNOON						SATURDAY AFTERNOON					
TOOTING BROADWAY	6 52	6 53	....	8 42	8 43	....	4 13	4 24	4 42		6 10	6 19	6 30	7 56		12 54	12 46	1 44	1 36	2 17	3 15
Southcroft Rd. *Mitcham Lane*		6 59	...		8 49	...	4 19	4 30			6 16		6 36			12 52		1 42	2 23	
Streatham *St. Leonards Ch.*		7 6	...		8 56		†4 27	4 37			6 23		†6 44			12 59		1 49	†2 31	
Clapham Common *Station*	7 5			8 55				4 56			6 33			8 10	11 37	1 8		1 58		3 29
Stockwell *Swan*	7 11	7 26	....	9 1	9 16		4 58	5 2			6 44	6 39			11 43	1 14	1 19	2 4	2 9	
Vauxhall *Station*	7 18	7 33		9 8	9 23		5 5	5 9			6 51	6 46			11 50	1 21	1 26	2 11	2 16	
SAVOY ST. *Embankment*	7 29	7 44		9 19	9 34		5 16	5 20			7 2	6 57			12 1	1 32	1 37	2 22	2 27	

†-Time at Streatham *Library*.

44. Thirty-three years on from 1917, and E/3 car 1966 is about to traverse the same length of track. The rise in the background is the bridge over the Brighton main line and the tram tracks on the bridge were laid close to the kerb on the south side. (John H.Meredith)

45. Mitcham Lane crossed the little River Graveney into Surrey, so, in order to remain in the County of London, the LCC tracks turned sharply westwards to follow a proposed new highway (later Southcroft Road). E/1 car 1004 has just turned left on its way to central London via Streatham. (Pat Loobey Coll.)

46. From the marks in the roadway, it appears that the sharp curve at what became known as Southcroft Corner, had caused some derailments. However, D class car 342 seems to have come safely to a stand. Service 14 operated from Wandsworth Depot and only ventured beyond Tooting (to Streatham Library) for a brief period in 1913/14 - this view is dated 13th November 1913. The car's indicator reads LATCHMERE ROAD, which is a short working destination along Battersea Park Road. (D.Jones Coll.)

47. Surprisingly the long Feltham cars could safely pass one another on the curve at Southcroft Corner, but here Feltham 2098 is passing E/3 car 1920. (John H.Meredith)

Tooting - Balham - Clapham - City *Southwark*

P.M. times are in heavy figures

Mitcham Road, Tooting High Street, Upper Tooting Road, Balham High Road, Balham Hill, Clapham Common South Side, Clapham High Street, ...ham Road, Kennington Park Road, Newington Butts, Newington Causeway, Borough High Street, Marshalsea Road, Southwark Bridge

...LWAY STATIONS SERVED : Tooting Broadway, Trinity Road, Balham, Clapham South, Clapham Common, Clapham *SR*, Clapham North, ...xwell, Oval, Kennington, Elephant & Castle, Borough

...ice interval : MONDAY to FRIDAY peak hours only 8 minutes, SATURDAY 8 minutes.

	MONDAY to FRIDAY										SATURDAY				
	MORNING				AFTERNOON										
	First			Last			First		Last			First			Last	
TING *Amen Corner* ..	5 15	5 21	..	8 49		..4 58	..		**6 16**	**7 51**	..	..	5 15	5 21	..	..	12 41	**2 9**	..
...ting *Broadway*	5 17	5 23	..	8 51			**5 0**	..	**6 18**	**7 53**	..	....	5 17	5 23	..	..	12 43	**2 11**	..
...ham Common *Station*	5 35	5 41	..	9 5		**3 44**	**5 16**	..	**6 34**	**8 9**	..	..	5 35	5 41	..	..	12 58	**2 26**	..
...nington *Gate*	5 47	5 53	..	9 15		**3 55**	**5 27**	....	**6 43**		...	...	5 47	5 53	..	..	**1 9**		..
...Y *Southwark*	6 1	6 9	..	9 29		**4 9**	**5 43**		**7 1**			..	6 1	6 9	..	..	**1 24**		..
...Y *Southwark*		6 3		8 7	9 31		**4 11**		**7 3**					6 3		..	**1 25**		
...nington *Gate*		6 17		8 21	9 45		**4 27**		**7 19**					6 17		..	**1 40**		
...ham Common *Station*	4 53	6 27		8 31	9 55		**4 38**		**7 30**				4 53	6 27		..	**1 51**		
...ting *Broadway*	5 11	6 41		8 45	..		**4 54**		**7 45**		..		5 11	6 41		..	**2 6**		
...TING *Amen Corner*	5 13	6 43		8 47	...		**4 56**		**7 48**		...		5 13	6 43		..	**2 8**		

*—Special journey.

48. After the First World War a large LCC housing estate was built around Southcroft Road, but
prior to this, the tram route remained in isolation crossing open land without even the carriageway
or the footpaths having been constructed. This location was consequently known as "The Prairie" or
"The Klondyke"! Unfortunately it has not been possible to trace any photographs from this period.
This view is looking back along Southcroft Road near its junction with the Mitcham Road route at
Amen Corner. Feltham 2158 is working on route 8, whilst E/3 car 204 is returning to Telford Avenue
Depot to complete its working on peak hours only route 22.
(John H. Meredith)

49. This imposing parade of shops is at Amen Corner and stands between the Streatham line on the
left and the Tooting Junction line on the right. Route numbers (or as the LCC termed them: "service
numbers") were introduced in 1912, and for about a year were displayed under the canopy. D class
car 397 has such a canopy fitting and is rostered on route 12 from Tooting Junction to Hop Exchange
via Garratt Lane.   (Pat Loobey Coll.)

50. On Saturday, 28th July 1923, King George V and Queen Mary visited the Borough of Wandsworth to open Southfields Park, which was renamed King George's Park in honour of the occasion. The royal visitors later toured parts of the borough and we observe here some of the large crowds gathering to watch the proceedings. Photographed from the parade of shops seen in the previous view, E/1 car 1530 is on service 6, which at this time linked Southcroft Corner and Southwark Bridge. (Pat Loobey Coll.)

51. The tracks towards Tooting Junction were closed in September 1937 when trolleybuses took over from Battersea to Mitcham (route 612) and Willesden Junction to West Croydon (route 630). Trams continued to serve Southcroft Road for nearly fourteen years. On 29th May 1950 Feltham car 2087 stands at the site of the junction whilst car 2 is in the distance. A new style tram stop sign has recently been provided, much like the bus stop pattern, but in blue instead of red. (John H.Meredith)

52. In 1926 LCC trams were extended over South Metropolitan tracks from Tooting Junction to Mitcham. A plough change was provided just south of Amen Corner, but cars going only as far as the former Tooting Junction terminus were able to retain their ploughs. In this scene from around 1936, E class car 439 has come through from Mitcham and is taking up its plough. (K.H.Rudolph)

53. Well before the 1926 through running at Tooting Junction, open top D class car 391 stands at the LCC terminus in Mitcham Road on the north side of the railway bridge. Across the county boundary on the Surrey side stands SMET bogie car 27 at that company's terminus in London Road. (Pat Loobey Coll.)

54. Facing in the opposite direction in 1911, SMET car 32, a former Gravesend and Northfleet tramcar (fully described in *North Kent Tramways*), and LCC D class car 335, are standing at their respective termini. The SMET route had opened in 1906 and the LCC arrived here in the following year. (Pat Loobey Coll.)

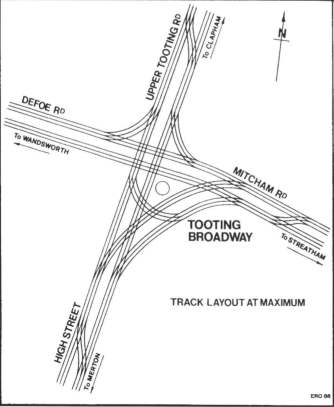

TRACK LAYOUT AT MAXIMUM

ERO 88

55 and 56. These two photographs give an insight into the complexities of the construction of the LCC's conduit track as work progresses in Mitcham Road, Tooting during 1907. Long yokes tie the running rails together, yet at the same time allow for an unobstructed conduit, whilst intermediate short yokes preserve the continuity of the conduit slot. The fearsome appliance is referred to as a "Jim Crow" and is used for curving or straightening rails as required.
(55: Lens of Sutton,
56: John B. Gent Coll.)

Reproduced from *LCC Tramways Volume 1 (London Tramways History Group)*, courtesy of E.R.Oakley.

57. From an elevated viewpoint, this scene is looking west along Mitcham Road towards Tooting Broadway. The large building with a prominent cupola is the Tooting Central Methodist Hall and can be seen from the opposite direction in illustration 60. An E class tramcar is approaching, closely followed by an LGOC B type bus. (Pat Loobey Coll.)

58. On 11th November 1950 rehabilitated E/1 car 1357 has just left Tooting Broadway terminus at the start of its journey to the city at Southwark Bridge. In common with other "rehabs" the car's three line route indicator has been partly obscured to enable it to take the two line blinds as used on standard cars. The junction in the trolleybus overhead provides access to a turning circle in Longmead Road. (John H.Meredith)

59. A right angle crossing of the two double track lines was all that existed when the tramways were laid at Tooting Broadway in 1905/07. This scene from Mitcham Road looking across the junction to Defoe Road and Garratt Lane shows D class car 418 on a working to Latchmere Road. Behind the island on the left is a tram on the Clapham route and two further trams can be seen on the Garratt Lane route in Defoe Road. (Lens of Sutton)

60. By 1919 a complex set of curves had been laid between the two routes and in this view from around 1930, E/1 car 1667 on route 4A passes Tooting Broadway Station having diverged left from Mitcham Road, and is about to turn right into Upper Tooting Road. Routes 2A and 4A worked from Streatham Library to the Embankment via Tooting, but were permanently withdrawn as part of the wartime cutbacks in 1942. (Pat Loobey Coll.)

61. At the same location as the previous view, E/1 car 1532 on route 20 is performing a similar manoeuvre on 25th July 1948, but its ultimate destination is Victoria rather than the Embankment. Note the relics of the three lamp indicators which gave a colour code in the days before route numbers. Also evident is an elderly LT type bus which would be withdrawn before the year was out, and a trolleybus. The double track curve from Mitcham Road to Tooting High Street had by then fallen into disuse; its only regular service is thought to have been in 1914/16. (B.T.Cooke)

62. On 3rd June 1950, the conductor of Feltham car 2106 puts out his arm, as this route 8 tram negotiates the curve from Upper Tooting Road into Mitcham Road. Services 8 and 20 from Victoria were complementary: the 8 taking an anti-clockwise circle from Stockwell via Clapham, Tooting, Streatham and Brixton, while the 20 took a clockwise course. Note the blanked off front exit stop light to the left of the masked headlamp. (A.B.Cross)

63. Two E class cars are seen in Defoe Road in this view looking towards Tooting Broadway around 1910. Both cars display the destination PLOUGH ROAD which is a short working point in York Road, Wandsworth. (Lens of Sutton)

64. Defoe Road later became part of Garratt Lane, and on 6th June 1949, Feltham car 2107 has just reversed and is picking up passengers prior to its return journey to central London on route 10. Behind car 2107, a Wimbledon bound E/1 on route 4 is about to cross the Tooting Broadway Junction. (John H.Meredith)

65. The date is 11th November 1950 and a Norwood Depot "rehab" E/1 car 1514 reverses on the Garratt Lane crossover beneath trolleybus overhead and power feed wires. The rails beyond the crossover have been lifted and trolleybuses reign supreme. (John H.Meredith)

SUMMERSTOWN AND GARRATT LANE

A quarter mile line along Wimbledon Road to Summerstown was opened in 1910. The route was laid with a triangular junction at Garratt Lane; at Summerstown it met the London United Tramways Haydons Road route which was inaugurated in 1907. An initial service from St.George's Church to Summerstown via Streatham was very short lived and the line then seems to have existed on an "as required" basis. However in 1931, the LCC took over the LUT route, the two lines were connected and a change pit installed. Route 14 was then revised to work from Hop Exchange to Wimbledon via Embankment, Wandsworth and Summerstown. A greyhound stadium with capacity for 20,000 spectators was built at Summerstown in 1933, and this gave rise to additional traffic with special cars being provided. Route 14 was withdrawn in 1934 and the tracks in Haydons Road were abandoned, however, a tramway connection from the stadium to Tooting remained until 1939 when the stadium branch was wired for trolleybuses. However, a tramway connection from the Stadium to Tooting remained until 15th January 1940 when trolleybuses took over the Stadium Branch.

66. No photographs of the LCC or London Transport operations on the Summerstown branch have come to light, hence this scene of an LUT car on the Haydons Road route. Further views of this line are included in *Kingston and Wimbledon Tramways*. (Pat Loobey Coll.)

67. In Garratt Lane another group of young people pose for the camera. This view is a quarter of a mile south of Earlsfield Station with Isis Street on the left and St. Andrew's Church on the right, just past the tramcar. Garratt Lane is a somewhat unprepossessing thoroughfare with few noteworthy buildings which has resulted in a corresponding dearth of good pictures. (Pat Loobey Coll.)

68. Facing south, the slender spire of St. Andrew's Church is immediately behind the tram which is D class car 345 en route to Hop Exchange. This scene was little changed in 1997; unfortunately only the trams were missing. (B.J. Cross Coll.)

69. At Earlsfield Station bridge the tramway tracks were laid close to the west abutment in order to avoid road widening and bridge reconstruction costs. A tramcar can be seen in the distance and an LSWR M7 class 0-4-4T is pulling a "down" local train away from the station which is also featured in the Middleton Press volume *Waterloo to Woking*. (John B.Gent Coll.)

70. Taken soon after the 1906 opening of the Garratt Lane route, the photographer is standing under the Earlsfield railway bridge and is looking north. Open top D class car 384 is unusual in that its reversed stairs have been replaced with normal direct ones. All LCC double deck cars were eventually so equipped, but practically all had to wait until fully enclosed top covers were fitted. (Lens of Sutton)

71. The sender of this postcard view, franked 16th October 1908, has marked with a cross the shop over which he was living. On the tramway front, an open balcony D class car is approaching. The building on the right - originally constructed in 1902 as an orphanage - must be the most impressive in Garratt Lane. It is at an angle to the main road and only the side is visible in this picture. (Pat Loobey Coll.)

72. The Garratt Lane/Wandsworth route was opened in 1906 and crossed Wandsworth High Street at the Ram Inn. However, it was not until 1915 that tracks were laid westwards along the High Street to connect with the line to Putney, Hammersmith and Willesden Junction. In 1921, the route was extended eastwards along the High Street to connect with the East Hill terminus of the Wandsworth Road route. This photograph shows car 424 crossing from Garratt Lane into York Road, with Young's Brewery dominating the skyline as it does to this day. (Pat Loobey Coll.)

STOCKWELL

73. At the Swan, Stockwell, the Brixton to Vauxhall route crossed the Clapham Road route and there were curves from both Vauxhall and Brixton towards Clapham Common, although the latter curve was not built until 1921. This view is facing south along Clapham Road, with Stockwell Underground Station on the far corner. This station, in 1890 the southern terminus of the world's first electric "tube" railway, is now an important interchange between the Northern and Victoria lines.   (Pat Loobey Coll.)

74. Feltham car 2143 and Daimler utility bus D79 have just turned from South Lambeth Road into Clapham Road at Stockwell Station. Note the *Evening News* delivery van - Londoners then had three evening papers to choose from, the other two being the *Evening Standard* and *The Star* - and the United Daries Scammel tractor and articulated trailer. The date is 14th October 1950. (John H.Meredith)

CLAPHAM

75. With no other mechanical transport in sight, an E class car (right) is bound for Clapham Common. The photographer has positioned himself in Clapham Road opposite Clapham North Underground Station then styled Clapham Road Station. (John B. Gent Coll.)

76. On 14th October 1950 at the same location as the previous view E/3 car 201 is shown in splendid isolation. There are no other vehicles in sight on this major South London highway - the A3! This particular tram is an ex-Leyton vehicle now attached to Telford Avenue Depot. (John H. Meredith)

Tramway Depôt

This extract from the OS map (1898 edition) shows the area around the Plough, Clapham. Prior to road widening for further electric tramways, the LCC engineers have annotated rateable values of adjoining properties.

P.H.

69·3

70·0

71·8

73·3

F.P.

73·5
L.B.

St. Mary's R.C. Church

H 4

Plough Hotel
(P.H.)

52·9

Drinking Fn.

T R A M W A Y

72·7

St. Mary's Monastery

Alexandra Hotel

77. The LCC's first electrified route, from the Thames bridges to Tooting, was opened with great pomp and ceremony. HRH The Prince of Wales undertook the formal opening and travelled in a white painted and lavishly furnished tramcar on 15th May 1903. Thousands lined the route as the car approached the Plough at Clapham Common.   (J.H.Price Coll.)

78. The route immediately settled down to its day to day business and, a few years later an A class car, fitted with a low height cover to the top deck (for more details see caption to picture 107), is seen outside Clapham Common Station. From this point northwards the trams competed with the City & South London tube railway which had been extended from Stockwell to Clapham Common in 1900. The "QUICKEST ROUTE TO THE WEST END" then involved changing at Bank on to a Central London Railway train!   (John H.Meredith Coll.)

79. Bomb damage has changed the scene as E/1 car 1565 on route 34 passes the site of the C&SLR station building in 1949. The rather forbidding structure on the right is an access and ventilation shaft to one of the deep air raid shelters which had been built below the tube railway tunnels with the intention of incorporating them later in a four tracking scheme to relieve overcrowding on the Northern Line. The C&SLR was by now part of this line with direct connections to the West End as well as the City - an extension southwards to Morden followed in 1926. (John H.Meredith)

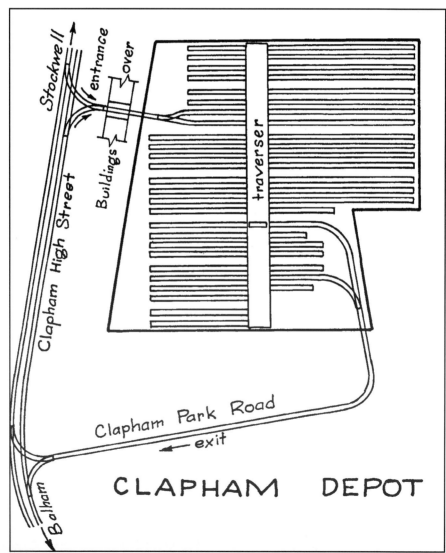

Stockwell

entrance

over

Buildings

traverser

Clapham High Street

Clapham Park Road

← exit

Balham

CLAPHAM DEPOT

80. Clapham Depot was built behind existing buildings, part of the site having previously been used as a horse tram depot. It had a narrow entrance from Clapham Road which passed through a parade of shops. Inside the depot in about 1938 several unvestibuled E/1s are to be seen. Note the continuous pits with protected side conduits and the cleaning trollies. (Jack Turley)

81. In this early 1945 view, E/1 car 1484 is serving as a static first aid post to deal with injuries from air raid incidents. Apart from Norwood, all the London tram depots suffered bomb damage and many tramcars were destroyed. (John H.Meredith)

82. E/1 car 1802 emerges from the depot exit into Clapham Park Road to enter peak hour service on route 22 in 1949. Note the illuminated BEWARE OF CARS CROSSING warning sign. (John H.Meredith)

83. In June 1949, "rehab" car 1770 leaves the depot on route 26, but the route number blind appears to be missing. Route 26 (Clapham Junction - Hop Exchange) had normally worked from Wandsworth Depot, but operation was transferred to Clapham in 1949 to provide space at Wandsworth for conversion of the depot to a bus garage. Clapham Depot was itself converted to a bus garage but its life in that role was short, and it then served as the Museum of British Transport prior to the setting up of the present museums at Covent Garden and York. It housed some of London's preserved tramcars as well as some from further afield such as a Douglas horse car. (John H.Meredith)

84. The Metropolitan Street Tramways Company opened their horse tramway from Kennington to the Plough, Clapham Common in 1871, and it was later extended to Tooting. In this view at the Plough the loop line used for terminating cars at this busy point can be seen. The loop was perpetuated in the electric era, but was removed in the 1920s. (J.H.Price Coll.)

85. Efforts were made to keep horse trams running while electrification proceeded. This picture shows two horse trams, now under LCC ownership, on the new conduit tracks at Clapham Common. The date is January 1903.   (F.Merton Atkins Coll.)

86. Two new A class cars, 14 and 60, are seen at the Plough still with route details painted on the canopy bends. Note that car 60 is terminating at the Plough and will presumably reverse on to the loop line before returning to central London.   (Pat Loobey Coll.)

87. The clock tower at Clapham was presented by Alexander Glegg, Mayor of Wandsworth 1905/06. The inauguration by the Lord Mayor of London, Sir Walter Vaughan Morgan, took place after he had been driven in state from the City. Seen here during the formal ceremony on 19th July 1906, is E class car 446, one of a class of 300 vehicles all built in 1906 (described fully in *Stamford Hill Tramways*) and the first LCC cars to have covered tops from the outset.   (John B.Gent Coll.)

(lower left)
88. This view shows two cars northbound at the Plough around 1914. By this time the operation of the conduit was working comparatively well, perhaps too well. Enormously expensive to install and subject to lengthy interruptions to services when failures did occur, London's tramway system might have had a greater chance of survival, at least in part, if the overhead system had been employed more generally.   (John B.Gent Coll.)

89. When the loop at Clapham Common was removed, cars had to reverse instead over a crossover in Long Road. A loading island was provided in the main road and here "rehab" car 1377, operating from Camberwell Depot on route 34, is about to turn right into Long Road. This tram is bound for Clapham Junction, Battersea Bridge and Kings Road, Chelsea. The car was one of a batch allocated to the twin wire Woolwich, Eltham and Lee Green section, and still retains double trollies, but now permanently "positive".   (John H.Meredith)

90. Our final scene at Clapham Common shows a variety of tramcars and services in 1949. On the left is Feltham car 2147 on route 8, whilst on the extreme right is 1922 Brush built E/1 car 1785 on route 6, followed by E/1 car 1049 on route 34. This car was one of fifty E/1s built by the LCC in 1907/08; another of this batch, car 1025, was appropriately selected for preservation. Apart from a handful of experimental or prototype cars, all other LCC tramcars were supplied by outside contractors. (John H.Meredith)

91. A turning circle was laid at The Avenue, close to Nightingale Lane at the southern extremity of Clapham Common. It was constructed to simplify the turning back of tramcars hauling trailers. Following the end of trailer operation in 1922, the circle became redundant and in this 1950 photo most of the point and crossing work had been removed. E/1 car 1826 is bound for Wimbledon on route 4; a new Leyland RTL bus is following and a wartime utility Daimler can also be seen with its customary opaque panel in the upper deck rear window space. (John H.Meredith)

92. E/1 car 1797 on route 8 is approaching Clapham South Underground Station in 1950, and by now a loading island has been provided for northbound passengers. The station building is just out of sight to the left of the photograph and the structures seen in the centre are associated with another deep level air raid shelter. (John H.Meredith)

93. Facing in the opposite direction, and soon after the 1903 opening of the electric tramway, A class cars 40 and 43 are about to pass at the top of Balham Hill. (John B.Gent Coll.)

BALHAM

94. Balham Hill falls quite steeply from Clapham South towards Balham. Of the three E or E/1 cars in this view, the tram on the left appears to be one of the first batch of E class cars which were built without draught screens to the upper deck.   (John B.Gent Coll.)

95. From virtually the same vantage point as the previous view, four tramcars are in similar juxtaposition, but this time all four are E/1s from the 1777 to 1851 series built in 1922. The date is 5th August 1950. (Pamlin Prints)

96. This rare postcard view shows car 30, one of the few A class cars to be fitted with low top covers which did not extend over the balconies - see also pictures 78 and 107. The magnificent Royal Duchess Palace Theatre stood at the corner of Balham Hill and Yukon Road. It later became the Balham Hippodrome, but was destroyed by bombing in the Second World War, and the site is now occupied by a block of flats. The carter appears to be attacking his horse with quite unnecessary vigour; unfortunately a not uncommon sight in those days.
(Pat Loobey Coll.)

97. Balham High Road developed into an important shopping centre and in this busy scene looking north from Balham Station, there are two E class cars, 474 on route 2 and 414 on route 6, and a new LGOC B type bus. The route number stencils below the canopy bends date this picture to about 1912/13. (B.J.Cross Coll.)

98. E/1s from the 1922 series are very much in evidence. Nearer the camera is 1784 on route 8 bound for Mitcham Cricket Green in SMET territory and it is followed by car 1788 on route 6 (John B.Gent Coll.)

99. By 1948 some new shops had been built but the trams are still running. Car 1805 is in quite smart condition, its body having received external bracing; it still retains the blue and white OAKEY'S enamelled advertisement panel. The tram certainly dwarfs the little Morris Commercial. (R.F.Mack)

ROUTES 2/4 — Wimbledon - Tooting - Clapham - Savoy Street

P.M. times are in heavy figures

Via Wimbledon Broadway, Merton Road, Merton High Street, Tooting High Street, Upper Tooting Road, Balham High Road, Clapham High Street, Clapham Road, Route 2 via Kennington Road, Westminster Bridge, Victoria Embankment, return via Blackfriars Bridge, Blackfriars Road, London Road, Newington Butts, Kennington Park Road, Route 4 via Kennington Park Road, Newington Butts, London Road, Blackfriars Road, Blackfriars Bridge, Victoria Embankment, return via Westminster Bridge, Kennington Road

RAILWAY STATIONS SERVED : Wimbledon, South Wimbledon, Colliers Wood, Tooting Broadway, Trinity Road, Balham, Clapham South, Clapham Common, Clapham SR, Clapham North, Stockwell, Oval, Lambeth North, Westminster, Charing Cross, Temple, Blackfriars, Elephant & Castle, Kennington

Service interval : 4-6 minutes

	WEEKDAYS First						MONDAY to FRIDAY Last						SATURDAY Last						SUNDAY First						Last			
WIMBLEDON Bdwy.	....	....	....	4 54	....	5 48	9 11	9 15	10 15	....			9 28	9 33	10 15	....				7 39	8 5	9 15	9 18	10 15		
Merton Change Pit	....	4 5	....	5 8	5 16	6 2	9 25	9 29	10 29	10 46	....		9 41	9 47	10 29	10 36	....		....	6 16	6 26	7 51	8 16	9 26	9 29	10 29	10 46
Tooting Broadway	....	4 6	4 32	5 9	5 17	6 3	9 26	9 30	10 30	10 47			9 42	9 48	10 30	10 37	11 21	4 7	....	6 17	6 27	7 52	8 17	9 27	9 30	10 30	10 47
Clapham Com. Station	4 15	4 19	4 45	5 25	5 33	6 16	9 40	9 46	10 46	11 3	....		9 58	10 4	10 46	10 53	11 37	4 23	5 4	6 30	6 40	8 4	8 30	9 41	9 46	10 46	11 3
Kennington Gate	4 25	4 29	4 55	5 37	5 45	6 26	9 52	9 58	....				10 10	10 16	....	....		4 33	5 14	6 40	6 50	8 14	8 40	9 53	9 58		
Elephant & Castle	4 31	4 35	....	5 43			....		10 5				....	10 23				4 38	....	6 55	8 19	....		....	10 5		
SAVOY ST. Embkt.	T4 43	T4 48	5 8	5 54	5 58	6 39	10 7	10 18					10 25	10 36				4 47	5 28	6 53	7 6	8 30	8 53	10 8	10 18		
SAVOY ST. Embkt.	....	T4 44	5 13	....			9 2	9 12	9 52	9 54	10 7	10 18	9 8	9 9	9 43	9 43	10 25	10 36	6 33	6 46	7 36	9 10	9 11	9 52	9 54	10 8	10 18
Elephant & Castle	....	4 57	....				9 15			10 7	10 20		9 21			9 56	10 38		6 46	....	7 47		9 23			10 7	10 21
Kennington Gate	....	5 4	5 28	....			9 22	9 27	10 7	10 14	10 27	10 33	9 27	9 23	9 58	10 3	10 45	10 51	6 51	6 59	7 52	9 24	9 28	10 7	10 14	10 28	10 33
Clapham Com. Station	3 46	4 21	5 16	5 40			9 33	9 39	10 19	10 26	10 39	10 45	9 38	9 34	10 10	10 15	10 57	11 3	7 1	7 9	8 2	9 39	10 19	10 26	10 40	10 45
Tooting Broadway	4 2	4 37	5 32	5 56			9 49	9 55	10 35	10 43		11 1	9 54	9 50	10 26	10 31	11 13	11 19	7 14	7 22	8 15	9 50	9 55	10 35	10 42		11 1
Merton Change Pit	4 3	4 38	5 33	5 57			9 50	9 56	10 36	10 44			9 55	9 51	10 27	10 32			7 15	7 23	8 16	9 51	9 56	10 36	10 43		
WIMBLEDON Bdwy.	....	4 52	5 47	6 11			10 4	10 10					10 9	10 5					7 34	8 27	10 5	10 10					

EARLY JOURNEYS—SUNDAY

Merton to John Carpenter Street at *5 29 a.m.
Merton to Savoy Street at †5 58 a.m.

Savoy Street to Merton at *4 48, *5 28, †5 43 a.m.
John Carpenter Street to Merton at *6 10 a.m.
Clapham Common to Tooting Broadway at 3 49 a.m.
Clapham Common to Merton at 5 41, 6 23, 6 39, 6 52 a.m.

LATE JOURNEY—MONDAY to FRIDAY and SUNDAY

Tooting to Clapham Common at 11 3 p.m.

*–Via Blackfriars. †–Via Westminster. T–Time at Charing Cross.

100. With Balham railway bridge in the background, HR/2 class car 1885 makes a photographic stop during a special tour for the Southern Counties Touring Society on 9th May 1948. An unusual visitor indeed for Balham, 1885 was one of four HR/2 cars included in the London Transport 1935 rehabilitation programme along with four ex-Croydon trams and some 150 E/1s. (John H.Meredith)

101. In the late 1930s E/1 car 1813 is in Balham High Road on route 2. The modern block of flats, Du Cane Court, contrasts with the still unvestibuled condition of the tramcar. The late provision of vestibule screens on London trams compared with most provincial cities was due largely to the attitude of the Metropolitan Police. (John H.Meredith Coll.)

102. Pending construction of the permanent depot at Clapham, the LCC converted the horse car sheds at Marius Road, Balham to house their first electric tramcars in May 1903. Four of the original A class cars, 22, 3, 37 and 4 are lined up behind the traverser pit.
(R.J.Harley Coll.)

103. Marius Road Depot was closed in 1904, but it enjoyed a new lease of operational life during the trailer car era - 1915 to 1922. Three petrol electric cars which had been employed on non-electrified routes in Rotherhithe, were adapted to shunt trailer cars in and out of the depot. This view was taken after trailer services had ceased and the cars were awaiting their fate. The 150 purpose built trailer cars were only six or seven years old, and many were sold for further use as dwellings or outhouses.
(F.Merton Atkins)

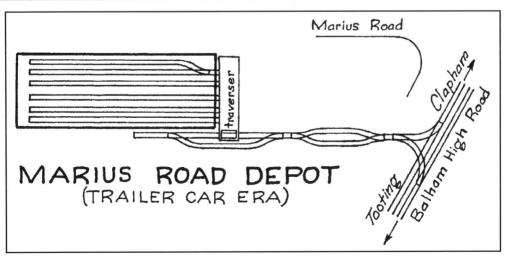

MARIUS ROAD DEPOT
(TRAILER CAR ERA)

104. Between Marius Road and Tooting Bec, "rehab" 1727 is seen on route 8 around 1937/38. Although the three line indicator boxes were generously proportioned, the setting of this particular destination display shows only the rather cryptic STATION - virtually useless for intending passengers! (R.J.Harley Coll.)

105. At the same location as the previous view, and probably on the same day, Feltham car 2134 is being pursued by two unvestibuled E/1s. (R.J.Harley Coll.)

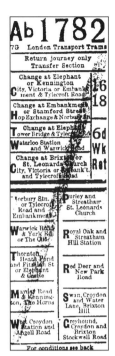

Dh 0269		
7H London Transport Trams		
Return journey only		
Transfer Section		
Change at Elephant or Kennington City, Victoria or Embankment & Tylecroft Road		16
Change at Embankment or Stamford Street Hop Exchange & Norbury Sn		18
Change at Elephant Tower Bridge & Tylecroft Rd		6d
Waterloo Station and Warwick Road		Wk
Change at Brixton or St. Leonards Church City, Victoria or Embank't and Tylecroft Road		Ret
Norbury Stn or Tylecroft Rd and Embankment		
Warwick Rd & York Rd or The Cut		
Th'rnt'n H'th Pd & Fitzal'n St or Elephant & Castle		
Mayday Rd. & Kenning ton, The Horns		
West Croydon Station & Angell Road		
Greyhound, Croydon and Brixton, Stockwell Rd.		

Lq 8885		
9D LONDON TRANSPT T&T		
1	8-20	20
2	10	19
3	16-18	18
4	22-24	17
5	42	16
5a	All N	15
6	Streat-ham and Thornton Heath Depots	14a
7		14
8	Issued subject to the bye-laws, conditions and regu-lations of the L.T. Executive in force at the time of issue.	13a
9		13
9a		12a
10	1½d, 2½d	12
10d	1d, 2d Ch.	11a
		11

Ne 7709		
A LONDON TRANSPT		
1	EXCHANGE TICKET	10
1½	To be issued only in exchange for a transfer ticket	10
2		9a
2½	Ticket available to point indicated by punch hole and must be shown or given up on demand. For further conditions see back.	9
3		8a
4		8
4½		7a
5		7
5½		6a
		6

Ab 1782		
7G London Transport Trams		
Return journey only		
Transfer Section		
Change at Elephant or Kennington City, Victoria or Embankment & Tylecroft Road		16
Change at Embankment or Stamford Street Hop Exchange & Norbury Sn		18
Change at Elephant Tower Bridge & Tylecroft Rd		6d
Waterloo Station and Warwick Road		Wk
Change at Brixton or St. Leonards Church City, Victoria or Embank't and Tylecroft Road		Ret
Norbury Stn. or Tylecroft Road and Embankment	Purley and Streatham St. Leonards Church	
Warwick Road & York Rd or The Cut	Royal Oak and Streatham Hill Station	
Thornton Heath Pond and Fitzalan St or Elephant & Castle	Red Deer and New Park Road	
Mayday Road & Kennington, The Horns	Swan, Croydon and Water Lane, Brixton Hill	
West Croydon Station and Angell Road	Greyhound, Croydon and Brixton Stockwell Road	

For conditions see back

106. The Metropolitan Street Tramways Clapham Road line eventually reached Tooting, Totterdown Street under the aegis of the London Tramways Company. The terminus was within 200 yards/182 metres of Tooting Broadway and the same location served as the original electric car terminus of 1903. The horse car here is southbound in Balham High Road near Ritherdon Road in 1899. (J.H.Price Coll.)

107. Some time around 1906 a coal cart has come to grief and blocked the northbound tram track in Balham High Road, about 300 yards/274 metres north of Trinity Road. By good fortune the incident was outside the premises of the American Studio at number 259 and one of their photographers recorded the scene on a picture postcard view. This is particularly fortuitous for the tramway historian. The Clapham route was affected by two low railway bridges - Clapham and Balham. When the LCC started to fit standard top covers to their A and D class cars, the bridges prevented their use on this route. In an attempt to overcome the problem, some six cars were equipped with low height covers

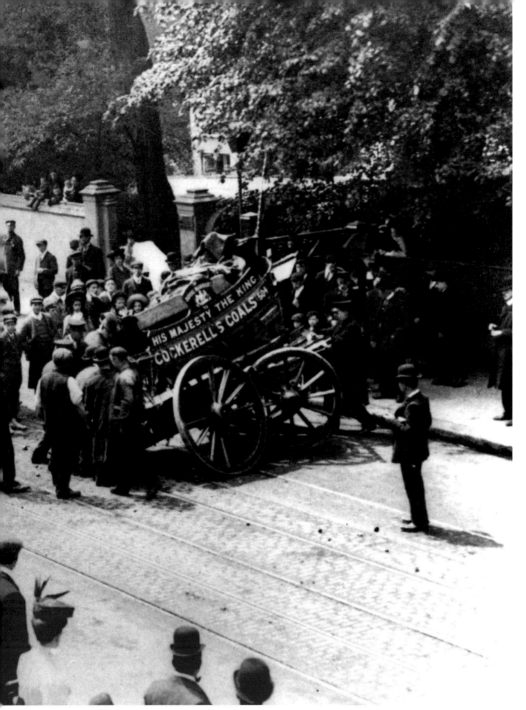

which did not extend over the balconies. The passengers here enjoying a grandstand view of the mishap from the front balcony, demonstrate very clearly the restricted headroom on the upper deck. However, the new E and E/1 class cars built from 1906 were lower and, provided they were without trolley poles, they could pass under the bridges. The earlier A and D class vehicles were then transferred elsewhere. Later route extensions required trolley fitted cars, so finally in 1922 the roadways under the two bridges were lowered. (Pat Loobey Coll.)

108. E/1 car 1525 has stopped at Trinity Road Underground Station in 1947 towards the end of the London Passenger Transport Board (LPTB) regime. Nationalisation took effect from 1st January 1948 and the organisation was then styled the London Transport Executive. Note the modern station building immediately to the left of the tram and the informative tram stop sign. In 1950 the station was renamed more appropriately Tooting Bec.   (John H.Meredith)

109. The Tooting route was extended from Totterdown Street to Tooting High Street in 1905. Not only can three A class cars be seen in this view, but there is also what appears to be the LCC's first non-passenger car. This was a street watering car built in 1904; unlike its successors it was never given a fleet number. The premises on the right later made way for Tooting Broadway Underground Station. (John B.Gent Coll.)

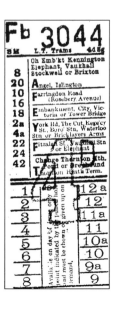

110. The route was extended again in 1907 by another half a mile to bring it to the London/Surrey boundary at Longley Road. Here the LCC met the LUT line from Wimbledon which had opened earlier in the same year. In the foreground LUT type W car 239 is standing at that company's "Tooting" terminus, while in the background are four E or E/1 cars working to the council's "Merton" terminus. Prominent signs direct those passengers from the LUT cars who wish to travel to Mitcham or Croydon, to take a brisk half mile walk along Longley Road to the SMET terminus at Tooting Junction!   (Pat Loobey Coll.)

LONG ROAD AND CEDARS ROAD

112. The first part of the tramway connecting link betwen Clapham and Wandsworth went along tree-lined Long Road through part of Clapham Common. Making its way in Long Road on 25th June 1949 is HR/2 car 1855. Prefabricated houses ("prefabs") can be seen to the right; these were put up in large numbers, even on common land as seen here, to overcome the housing shortage following the wartime bombing raids. A few still survive in parts of London.   (John H.Meredith)

111. In 1922 the LCC and LUT termini were connected. The LUT service was cut back and LCC cars worked through to Wimbledon or even to Hampton Court. To allow the LCC cars to work through on the overhead system, the conduit change pit seen here was installed. On 24th April 1948, car 1781 on route 2 is about to take up the plough as passengers board.   (John H.Meredith)

113. This photograph in Long Road is from 1912/13 with the car displaying service number 30 under the canopy. This service ran at that time from East Hill, Wandsworth to Waterloo Station. (John B.Gent Coll.)

ROUTE **34**	**Chelsea - Clapham - Camberwell - Blackfriars**		P.M. times are in heavy figures

Via Beaufort Street, Battersea Bridge, Battersea Park Road, Falcon Road, Lavender Hill, Cedars Road, Long Road, Clapham High Street, Clapham Road, Stockwell Road, Gresham Road, Coldharbour Lane, Denmark Hill, Camberwell Road, Walworth Road, London Road, Blackfriars Road, Blackfriars Bridge.

RAILWAY STATIONS SERVED : Clapham Junction, Clapham Common, Clapham SR, Clapham North, Stockwell, East Brixton, Loughborough Junction, Elephant and Castle Blackfriars.

Service interval : Chelsea–Camberwell, WEEKDAYS 4-6 mins., SUNDAY, morn. 12 mins., aft. and eve. 6 mins., Camberwell–Blackfriars, WEEKDAYS 12 mins. (peak hours 4 mins., Saturday afternoon 8 mins., evening 10-12 mins., SUNDAY 12 mins.

	WEEKDAYS First	SO	SX		SUNDAY First			DAILY Last	SO	
CHELSEA *Kings Road*	..	5 8	5 23	5 29		8 50	..	9 31	9 39	11 5
Clapham Junction	X4 46	5 8	5 20	5 35	5 41	8 19	8 59	9 43	9 51	11 17
Clapham Common *Stn., Underground*	4 7	4 51	4 58	5 18	5 39	5 43	5 51	†8 5	8 28	9 8	9 53	10 1	11 27
Brixton Road *Stockwell Road*	4 16	5 25	9 29	5 41	5 56	6 2	8 15	8 37	9 17	10 4	10 12
Camberwell Green	4 25	5 12	5 19	5 39	5 51	6 6	6 12	8 24	8 46	9 26	10 14	10 22
BLACKFRIARS *John Carpenter St.*	5 39	5 59	6 11	6 25	6 31	8 41	9 3	9 43	10 34

			First						Last		
BLACKFRIARS *John Carpenter St.*	..	5 40	6 0			8 43	....	10 0	10 36
Camberwell Green	4 28	6 0	6 19		8 48	9 0	10 20	10 56
Brixton Road *Stockwell Road*	4 37	6 10	6 29		8 57	9 9	10 30	11 6
Clapham Common *Stn., Underground*	4 39	4 46	6 19	5 38	9 6	9 18	10 41	11 17
Clapham Junction	X4 44	4 56	6 29	6 48	9 15	9 27	10 51
CHELSEA *Kings Road*	5 6	6 39	6 58	9 24	9 36	11 3

SO–Saturday only. SO–Sunday only. SX–Saturday excepted. X–Time at Battersea *Queenstown Road*.
†–Time at Clapham Common *Long Road*. *–Early journey.

EARLIER JOURNEYS–SUNDAY

Chelsea to Clapham Common at 6 57 a.m.
Chelsea to Brixton at 7 20 a.m.
Chelsea to Clapham Junction at 7 41 a.m.
Chelsea to Blackfriars at 8 1 a.m.
Chelsea to Stockwell at 8 22 a.m.
Clapham Common to Brixton at 6 41 a.m.
Clapham Common to Camberwell at 7 3, 7 51, 8 20, 8 28 a.m.
Clapham Junction to Clapham Common at 7 53 a.m.

Clapham Common to Chelsea at 6 37, 7 18 a.m.
Clapham Common to Clapham Junction at 8 8, 8 20, 8 35 a.m.
Camberwell to Clapham Junction at 7 24, 8 39 a.m.
Camberwell to Chelsea at 8 12 a.m.
Brixton to Chelsea at 6 51, 7 48 a.m.
Stockwell to Chelsea at 8 47 a.m.
Clapham Junction to Chelsea at 7 51 a.m.

114. The track in Long Road extended for about half a mile from the junction at Clapham Common, and then made a ninety degree turn into Cedars Road, flanked by the two impressive but gaunt residential buildings, landmarks to this day. The route opened in 1910, so the tramcars were relative newcomers when this photo was taken. (Pat Loobey Coll.)

115. Cedars Road was fairly level until the last few yards where it fell steeply to its junction with Wandsworth Road. There were some serious accidents at the bottom of this gradient and these are described in *Wandsworth and Battersea Tramways*. Car 501 prepares for the descent in this postcard view sent on 26th July 1911. (Pat Loobey Coll.)

ROLLING STOCK - Cable Cars

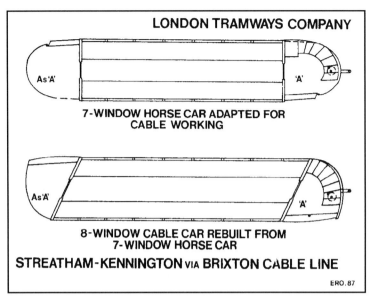

LONDON TRAMWAYS COMPANY

As 'A'   'A'

**7-WINDOW HORSE CAR ADAPTED FOR
CABLE WORKING**

As 'A'   'A'

**8-WINDOW CABLE CAR REBUILT FROM
7-WINDOW HORSE CAR**
STREATHAM-KENNINGTON via **BRIXTON CABLE LINE**

ERO. 87

Reproduced from *LCC Tramways Volume 1 (London Tramways History Group)*, courtsey of E.R.Oakley.

116. Apart from a network of horse tram routes stretching from Tooting to Greenwich, the London Tramways Company operated a cable tramway from Brixton to Streatham. Initially, horse cars were hauled along the cable section by special "dummy" gripper cars, and in this view the crews of the gripper and attendant passenger cars are posing outside the depot at Telford Avenue. (J.H.Price Coll.)

117. To eliminate the expense and inconvenience of having separate gripper cars, some horse trams were adapted to incorporate gripper mechanisms which could be disengaged at the changeover point where horses would take over. At the same time the car bodies were rebuilt with bulkheads that were not at right angles to the car sides. The LCC had secured control of the company in 1899, hence the inscription on the side of the car.
(London Transport Museum)

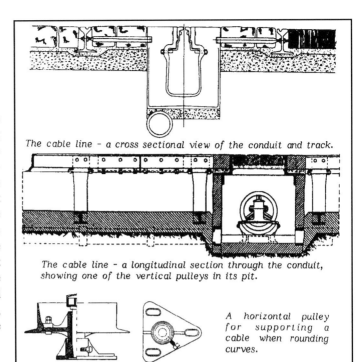

The cable line – a cross sectional view of the conduit and track.

The cable line – a longitudinal section through the conduit, showing one of the vertical pulleys in its pit.

A horizontal pulley for supporting a cable when rounding curves.

Trailer Cars

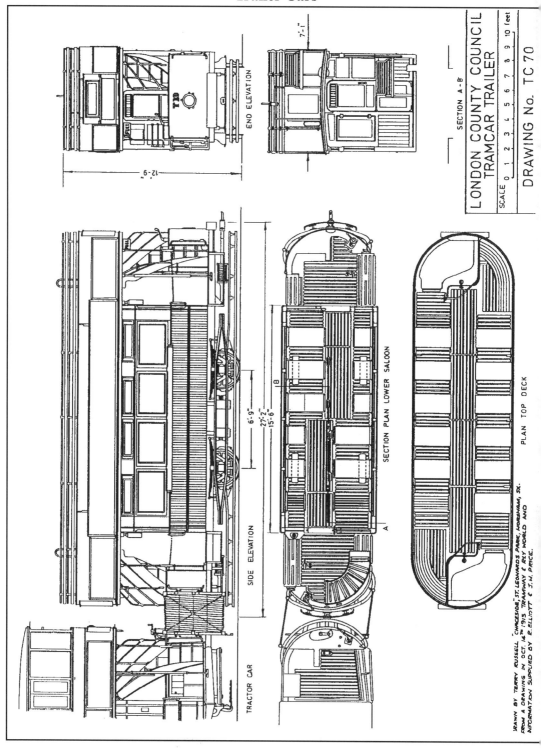

END ELEVATION

SECTION A - B

12'-9"

7'-1"

LONDON COUNTY COUNCIL
TRAMCAR TRAILER

SCALE 0 1 2 3 4 5 6 7 8 9 10 feet

DRAWING No. TC 70

SIDE ELEVATION

6'-9"
27'-2"
15'-6"

B

A

SECTION PLAN LOWER SALOON

TRACTOR CAR

PLAN TOP DECK

DRAWN BY TERRY RUSSELL "CHACESIDE" ST. LEONARDS PARK, HORSHAM, SX.
FROM A DRAWING IN OCT. 14TH 1915 TRAMWAY & RLY WORLD AND
INFORMATION SUPPLIED BY P. ELLIOTT & J.H. PRICE.

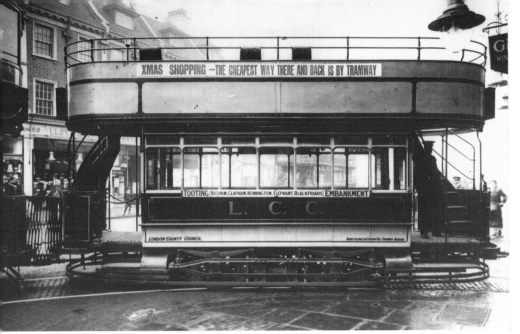

118. Eight converted horse trams were used for the initial experiments with trailer operation and were numbered T1 to T8. Note the new truck, extended canopies and raised decency panels. (J.H.Price Coll.)

119. The 150 purpose built trailer cars were constructed by Brush in 1915/16. They were allocated numbers T9 to T158. Here T116 is seen at St.Leonard's Church, Streatham in August 1916. (O.J.Morris)

"Clapham" E/1 Class

120. One thousand E/1 class cars were built for the LCC tramways between 1907 and 1922, with the final seventy-five (1777 to 1851) allocated to Clapham Depot for almost the whole of their existence. This final batch was generally similar to the pre-war cars, but had a modified front window arrangement on the upper deck. Each tram came equipped with two trolley poles. Car 1779 is seen here at the Victoria Embankment on all night service 1. This was a circular route via Clapham, Tooting and Streatham or vice versa. All night services had not previously carried route numbers, but were given them in 1946, including odd numbers 1, 3, 5 and 7. (D.W.K.Jones)

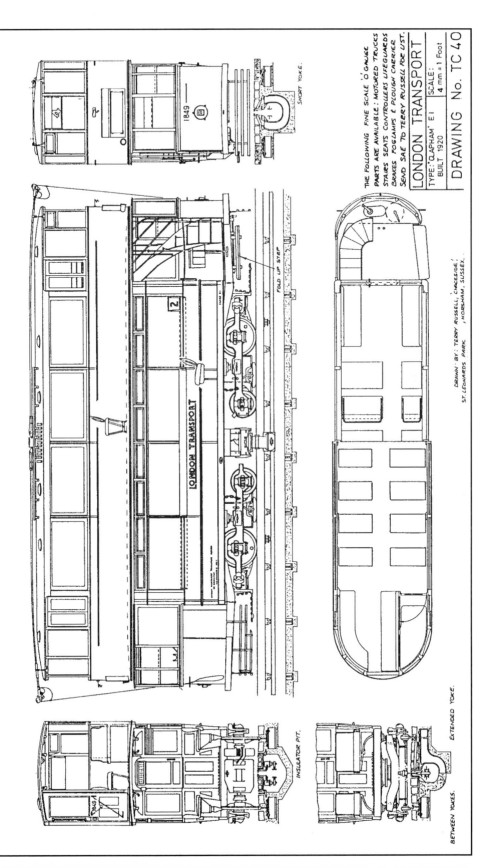

CAR FLEET No. 1727 - 1851

SHORT YOKE.

FOLD UP STEP

LONDON TRANSPORT

2

THE FOLLOWING FINE SCALE 'O' GAUGE
PARTS ARE AVAILABLE : MOTORED TRUCKS
STAIRS SEATS CONTROLLERS LIFEGUARDS
BRAKES FOGLAMPS & PLOUGH CARRIER
SEND SAE TO TERRY RUSSELL FOR LIST.

LONDON TRANSPORT

TYPE: "CLAPHAM" E1 | SCALE:
BUILT 1920 | 4 mm = 1 Foot

DRAWING No. TC 40

DRAWN BY : TERRY RUSSELL , CHMCESIDE ;
ST. LEONARDS PARK , HORSHAM , SUSSEX.

INSULATOR PIT.

BETWEEN YOKES.

EXTENDED YOKE.

Works Cars Class L/1

121. LCC works car 013 belonged to class L/1. It formed, with its sister car 014, part of a two car set originally constructed for freight traffic during the First World War. After some years of neglect it re-emerged in 1925 as a rail grinder with two water tanks. This scene dates from September 1933 and depicts car 013, still in LCC brown livery, outside Bexley Depot. This useful vehicle, which was also employed as a snow plough, was finally scrapped at Walthamstow Depot on 3rd March 1938. (D.W.K.Jones)

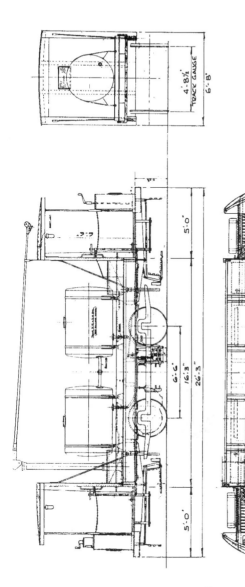

LONDON COUNTY COUNCIL TRAMWAYS
RAIL GRINDER & WATER CAR
CLASS L1 BUILT 1924   SCALE 4 MM = 1 FOOT
FLEET No 013-014
DRAWING No TC 563

4'-8½" TRACK GAUGE
6'-8"

5'-0"
6'-6"
16'-3"
26'-3"
5'-0"

SCALE
FEET 0 1 2 3 4 5 6 7 8 9 10 11 12

BY SEPTEMBER 1933 THE LIFEGUARD
GATES AND TRAYS HAD BEEN REMOVED
TO MAKE WAY FOR BEAM SNOWBOARDS
SET AT APPROX 45° TO THE FRONT.
THE CAR WAS SCRAPPED IN MARCH
1936 AT WALTHAMSTOW (DAVID BAVES)

MY THANKS TO ROY HUGGLE FOR PRODUCING THE ORIGINAL L.C.C BLUEPRINT FROM HIS ARCHIVE!

AVAILABLE FROM :- TERRY RUSSELL, "CHACESIDE", ST LEONARDS PARK, HORSHAM, W. SUSSEX. RH13 6EG.
SEND 3 FIRST CLASS STAMPS FOR COMPLETE LIST OF PUBLIC TRANSPORT DRAWINGS.

MP Middleton Press

Easebourne Lane, Midhurst. West Sussex. GU29 9AZ   Tel: 01730 813169 Fax: 01730 812601

..... Write or telephone for our latest list .....

BRANCH LINES

Branch Line to Allhallows
Branch Lines to Alton
Branch Lines around Ascot
Branch line to Ashburton
Branch Lines around Bodmin
Branch Line to Bude
Branch Lines around Canterbury
Branch Line to Cheddar
Branch Lines to East Grinstead
Branch Lines around Effingham Jn
Branch Line to Fairford
Branch Line to Hawkhurst
Branch Lines to Longmoor
Branch Line to Lyme Regis
Branch Line to Lynton
Branch Lines around Midhurst
Branch Line to Minehead
Branch Lines to Newport
Branch Line to Padstow
Branch Lines around Portmadoc 1923-46
Branch Lines around Porthmadog 1954-94
Branch Lines to Seaton & Sidmouth
Branch Line to Selsey
Branch Lines around Sheerness
Branch Line to Southwold
Branch Line to Swanage
Branch Line to Tenterden
Branch Lines to Torrington
Branch Line to Upwell
Branch Lines around Weymouth
Branch Lines around Wimborne

LONDON SUBURBAN RAILWAYS

Caterham and Tattenham Corner
Clapham Jn. to Beckenham Jn.
Crystal Palace and Catford Loop
East London Line
Holborn Viaduct to Lewisham
Lines aound Wimbledon
London Bridge to Addiscombe
Mitcham Junction Lines
North London Line
South London Line
West Croydon to Epsom
West London Line
Willesden Junction to Richmond
Wimbledon to Epsom

STEAMING THROUGH

Steaming through Cornwall
Steaming through East Sussex
Steaming through the Isle of Wight
Steaming through Kent
Steaming through West Hants
Steaming through West Sussex

GREAT RAILWAY ERAS

Ashford from Steam to Eurostar
Festiniog in the Fifties
Festiniog in the Sixties

COUNTRY BOOK

Brickmaking in Sussex

SOUTH COAST RAILWAYS

Ashford to Dover
Brighton to Eastbourne
Chichester to Portsmouth
Dover to Ramsgate
Ryde to Ventnor
Worthing to Chichester

SOUTHERN MAIN LINES

Bromley South to Rochester
Charing Cross to Orpington
Crawley to Littlehampton
Dartford to Sittingbourne
East Croydon to Three Bridges
Epsom to Horsham
Exeter to Barnstaple
Exeter to Tavistock
Faversham to Dover
Haywards Heath to Seaford
London Bridge to East Croydon
Orpington to Tonbridge
Sittingbourne to Ramsgate
Swanley to Ashford
Tavistock to Plymouth
Victoria to Bromley South
Waterloo to Windsor
Woking to Portsmouth
Woking to Southampton
Yeovil to Exeter

COUNTRY RAILWAY ROUTES

Bath to Evercreech Junction
Bournemouth to Evercreech Jn
Burnham to Evercreech Junction
Croydon to East Grinstead
East Kent Light Railway
Fareham to Salisbury
Frome to Bristol
Guildford to Redhill
Porthmadog to Blaenau
Reading to Basingstoke
Reading to Guildford
Redhill to Ashford
Salisbury to Westbury
Strood to Paddock Wood
Taunton to Barnstaple
Westbury to Bath
Woking to Alton

TROLLEYBUS CLASSICS

Croydon's Trolleybuses
Hastings Trolleybuses
Woolwich & Dartford Trolleybuses

TRAMWAY CLASSICS

Aldgate & Stepney Tramways
Bath Tramways
Barnet & Finchley Tramways
Bournemouth & Poole Tramways
Brighton's Tramways
Bristol's Tramways
Camberwell & W. Norwood Tramways
Clapham & Streatham Tramways
Croydon's Tramways
Dover's Tramways
East Ham & West Ham Tramways
Eltham & Woolwich Tramways
Embankment & Waterloo Tramways
Exeter & Taunton Tramways
Gosport & Horndean Tramways
Greenwich & Dartford Tramways
Hampstead & Highgate Tramways
Hastings Tramways
Holborn & Finsbury Tramways
Ilford & Barking Tramways
Kingston & Wimbledon Tramways
Lewisham & Catford Tramways
Maidstone & Chatham Tramways
North Kent Tramways
Portsmouth's Tramways
Reading Tramways
Seaton & Eastbourne Tramways
Southampton Tramways
Southend-on-sea Tramways
Stamford Hill Tramways
Thanet's Tramways
Victoria & Lambeth Tramways
Walthamstow & Leyton Tramways
Wandsworth & Battersea Tramways

OTHER RAILWAY BOOKS

Garraway Father & Son
Industrial Railways of the South East
London Chatham & Dover Railway

MILITARY BOOKS

Battle over Portsmouth
Battle Over Sussex 1940
Blitz Over Sussex 1941-42
Bognor at War
Bombers over Sussex 1943-45
Military Defence of West Sussex
Secret Sussex Resistance

WATERWAY ALBUMS

Hampshire Waterways
Kent and East Sussex Waterways
London's Lost Route to the Sea
London to Portsmouth Waterway
Surrey Waterways

BUS BOOK

Eastbourne Bus Story

SOUTHERN RAILWAY ● VIDEO ●

War on the Line